QUICK & EASY PICTURE CHORDS for GUITAR
by SAM MARTIN

This book contains all the chords you need to know to get started playing the guitar and it gives you the ability to play thousands of songs.

CONTENTS

Photos by James Bean, Ojai, CA
Photos of Roy Jones, Ventura, CA

Produced by John L. Haag

HAL•LEONARD® CORPORATION
7777 W. BLUEMOUND RD. P.O. BOX 13819 MILWAUKEE, WI 53213

Exclusively Distributed By

Visit Hal Leonard Online at
www.halleonard.com

How to Tune a Guitar

Tuning with a Piano:

To tune a guitar, turn the tuning pegs clockwise to raise or counter-clockwise to lower the pitch.
The pitch of the 6 strings of a guitar should match the pitch of the 6 keys shown on the keyboard.

Tuning by Strings:

1) Find the correct pitch for the 6th string.

2) Press the 5th fret of the 6th string - this pitch should match the open 5th string. (See Diagram)

3) Press the 5th fret of the 5th string - this pitch should match the open 4th string.

4) Press the 5th fret of the 4th string - this pitch should match the open 3rd string.

5) Press the 4th fret of the 3rd string - this pitch should match the open 2nd string.

6) Press the 5th fret of the 2nd string - this pitch should match the open 1st string.

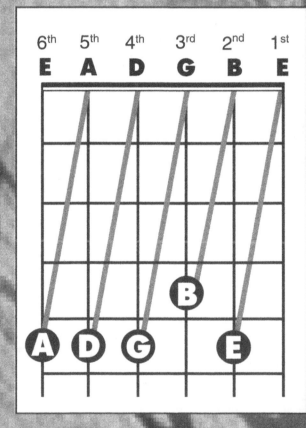

Tuning with Pitch Pipes:

Pitch pipes, which reproduce the correct pitch of each guitar string, are available at any music store.

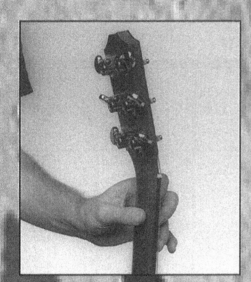

The Left Hand

Left Hand Position

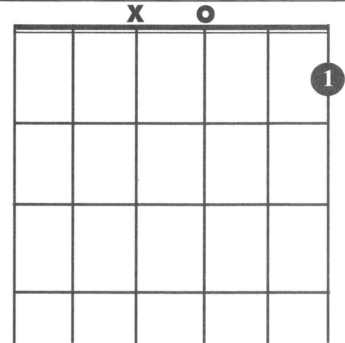

The notes that are being played

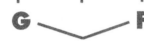

G   F

The vertical lines are the strings.
The horizontal lines are the frets.
The encircled number is the finger
    to use.
X = String is not to be played.
O = String is to be played open.

The Correct Way
To Hold The Guitar

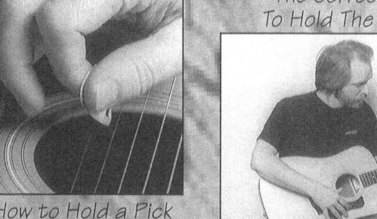

How to Hold a Pick

The Fingerboard

Do not use the palm of your hand to support
    the neck of the guitar.
Keep fingers arched.
Do not place the pick at the edge of the thumb.
Strike down with the pick.

Major Chords

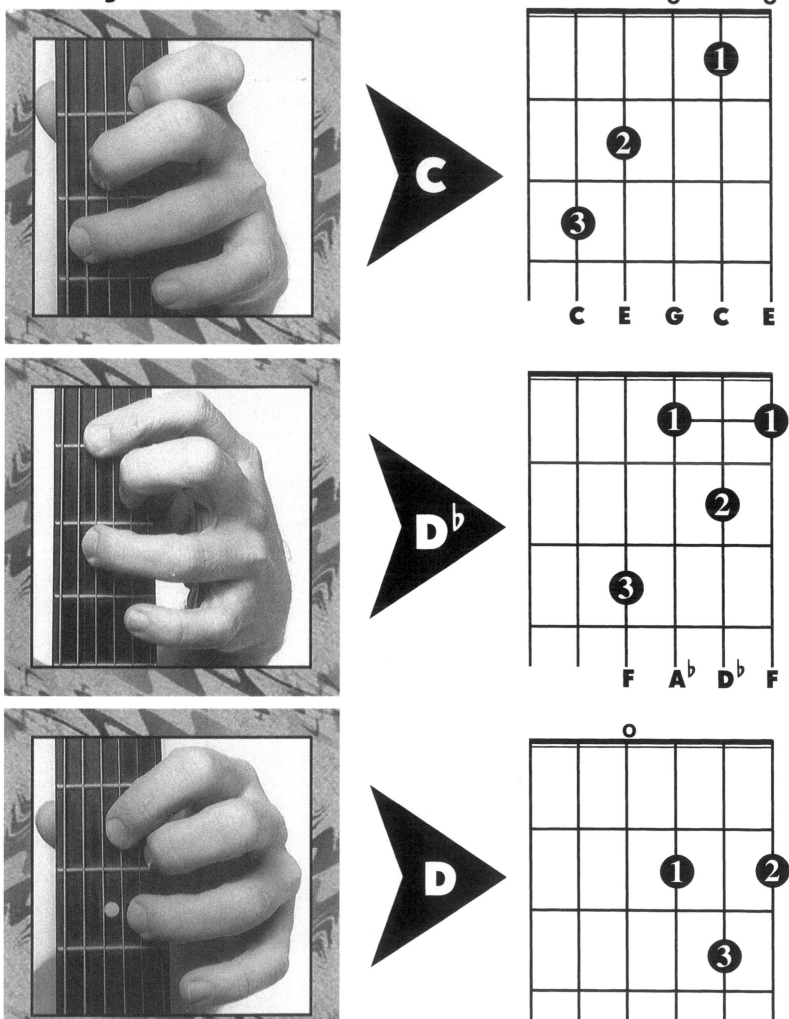

Major Chords

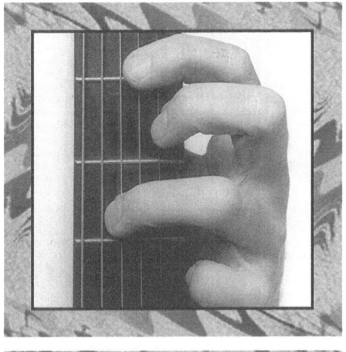

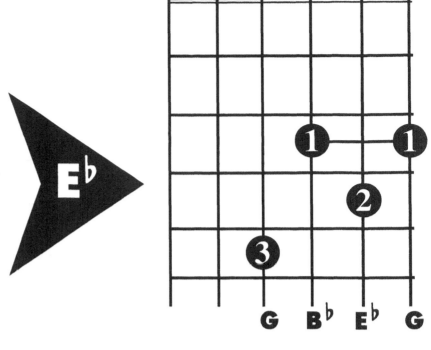

E♭

G   B♭   E♭   G

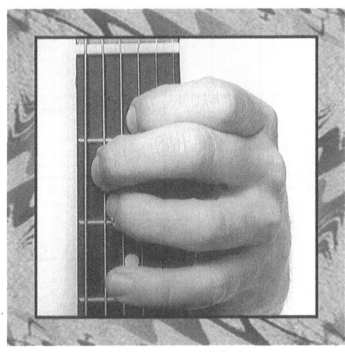

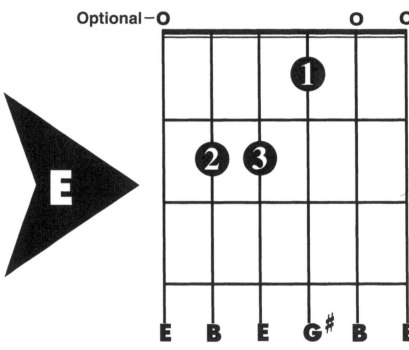

E

Optional—O

E   B   E   G#   B   E

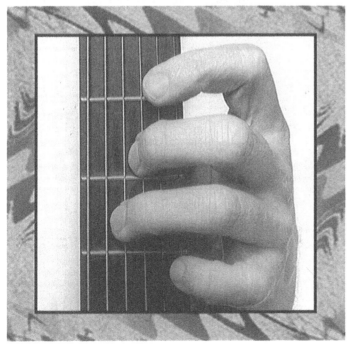

F

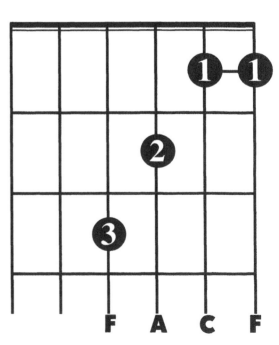

F   A   C   F

Major Chords

F#
Gb

F# A# C# F#

G

O   O   O

G   B   D   G   B   G

Ab

Ab C Eb Ab

Major Chords

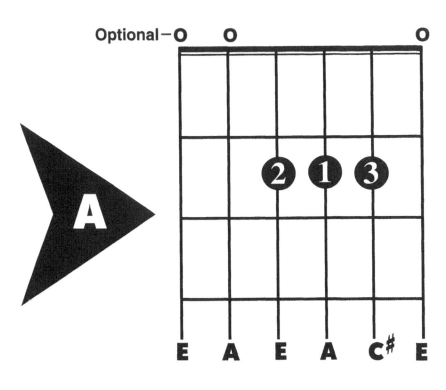

A

Optional—O O O

② ① ③

E A E A C# E

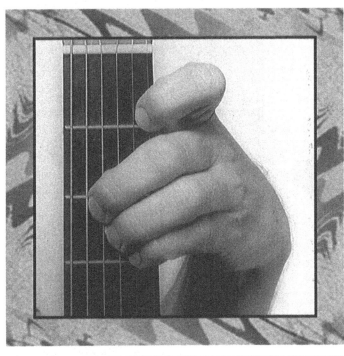

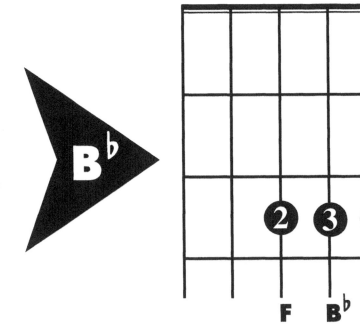

B♭

①

② ③ ④

F B♭ D F

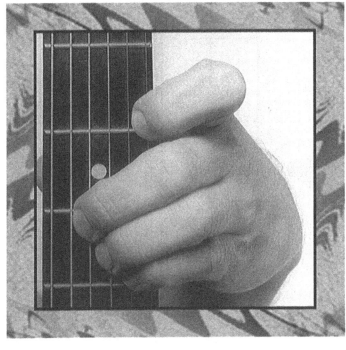

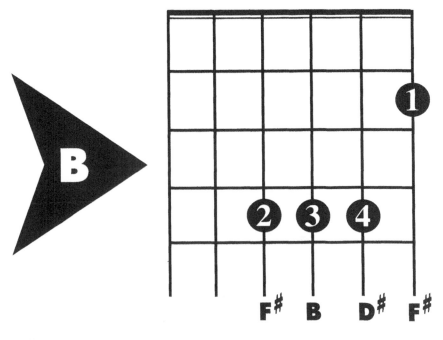

B

①

② ③ ④

F# B D# F#

Minor Chords (m)

Cm

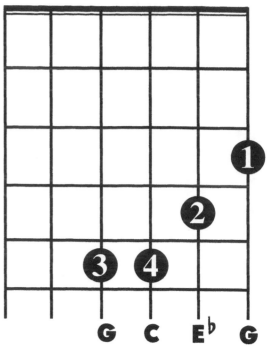

❶			
	❷		
❸	❹		

G   C   E♭   G

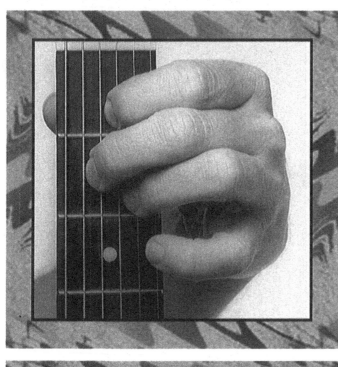

D♭m

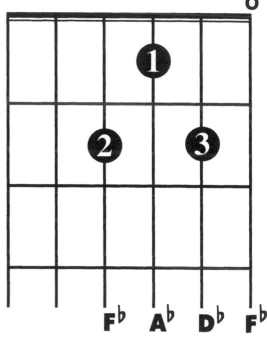

O

❶
❷   ❸

F♭   A♭   D♭   F♭

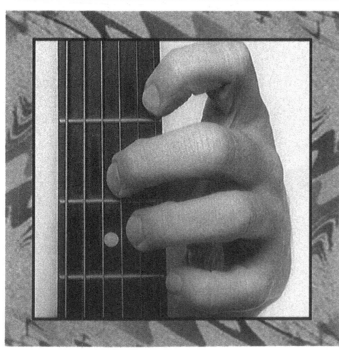

Dm

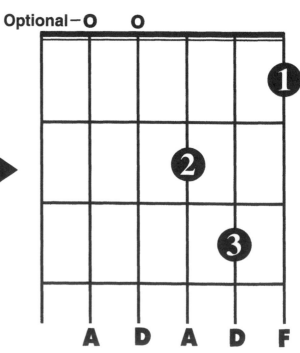

Optional—O   O

❶
❷
❸

A   D   A   D   F

8

Minor Chords (m)

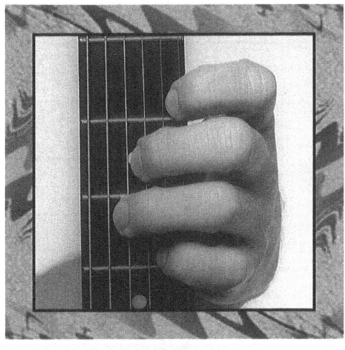

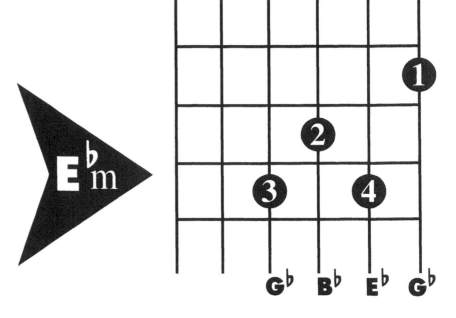

E^b_m

G♭ B♭ E♭ G♭

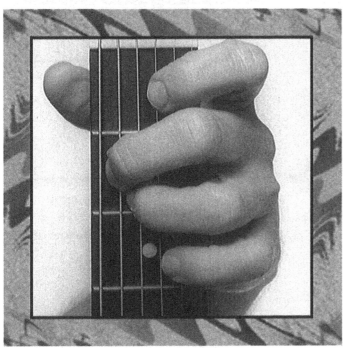

E_m

Optional—O   O   O   O

E B E G B E

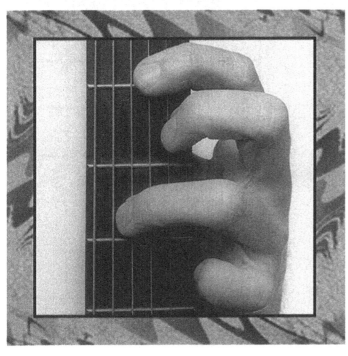

F_m

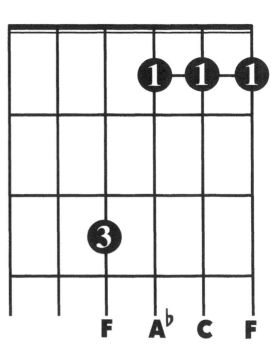

F A♭ C F

9

Minor Chords (m)

F#m
G♭m

F# A C# F#

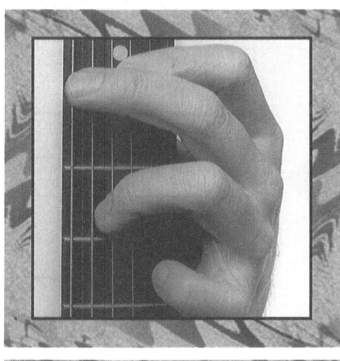

Gm

G B♭ D G

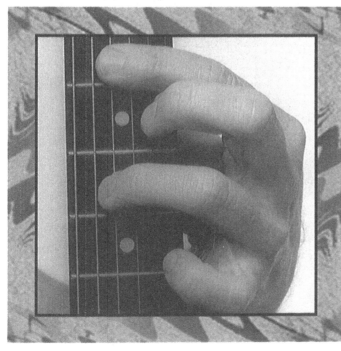

A♭m

A♭ C♭ E♭ A♭

Minor Chords (m)

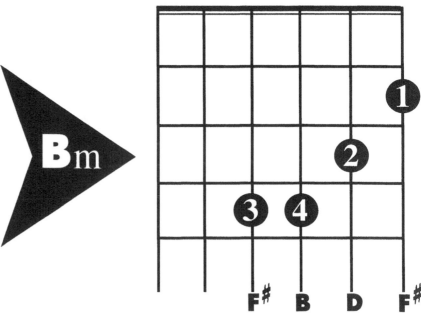

Am

E A E A C E

B♭m

F B♭ D♭ F

Bm

F# B D F#

11

Seventh Chords (⁷)

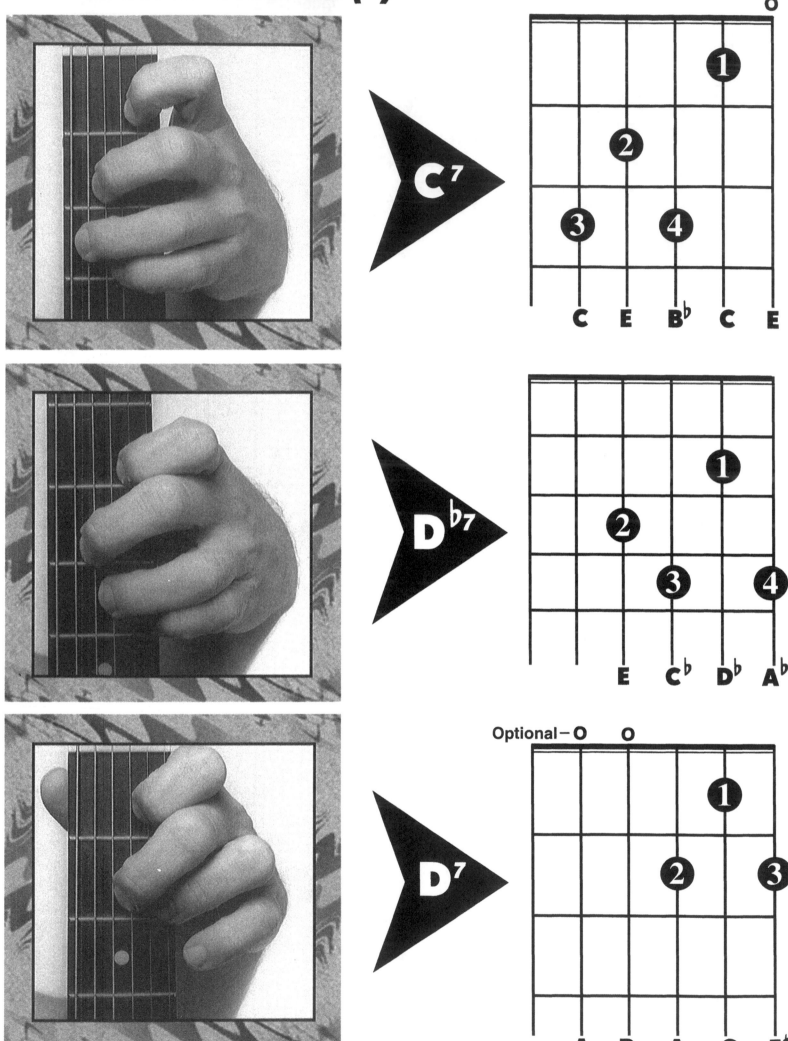

Seventh Chords (⁷)

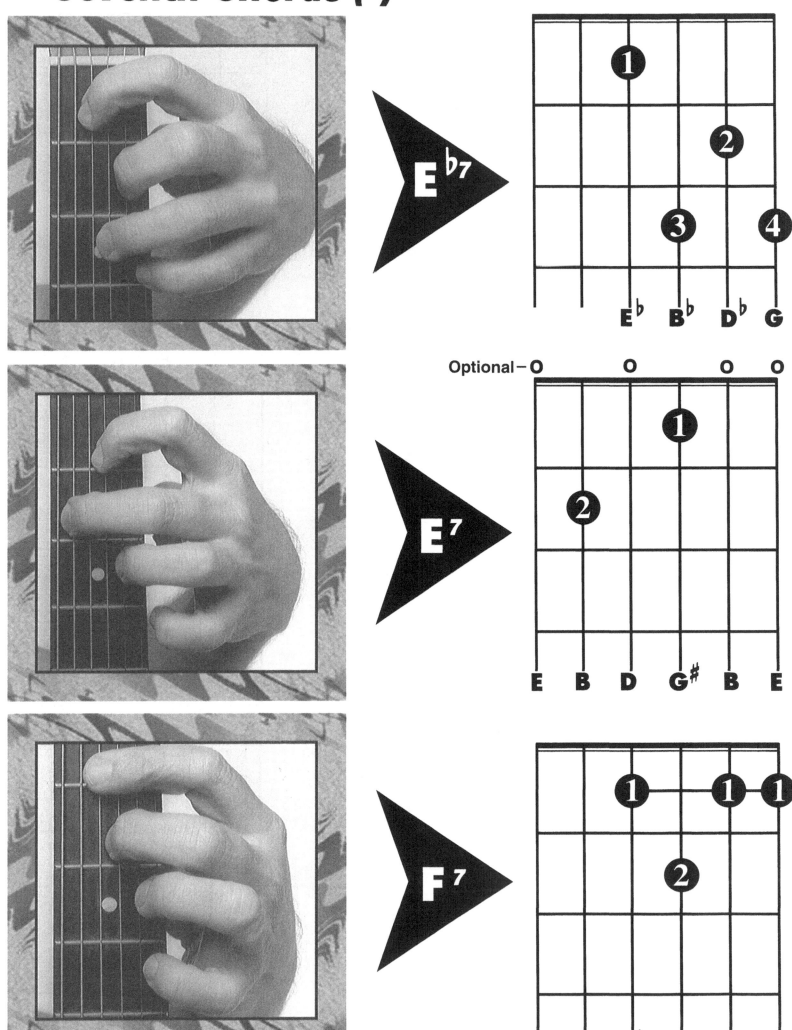

E♭⁷

E♭ B♭ D♭ G

Optional—O   O   O   O

E⁷

E B D G♯ B E

F⁷

E♭ A C F

Seventh Chords (⁷)

F#7
Gb7

O

① ② ③

F# A# C# E

G⁷

O O O

① ② ③

G B D G B F

Ab7

① ① ① ②

Eb Ab C Gb

Seventh Chords (⁷)

A⁷

E   A   E   A   C#   G

B♭⁷

F   B♭   D   A♭

B⁷

O

B   D#   A   B   F#

15

Diminished Chords (-)

D- A♭-
B- F-

o   o

① ②

D A♭ B F

E♭- A-
F#- C-
G♭-

① ②
③ ④

E♭ A C F#
              G♭

E-
B♭-
D♭-
G-

① ②
③ ④

E B♭ D♭ G

Augmented Chords (+)

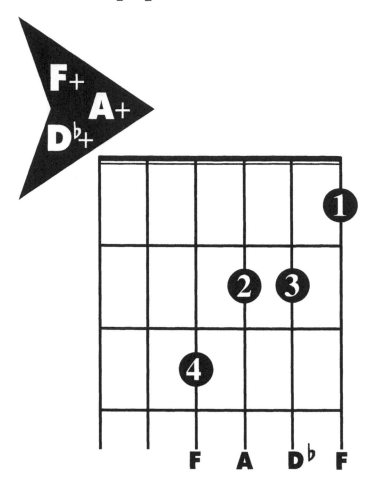

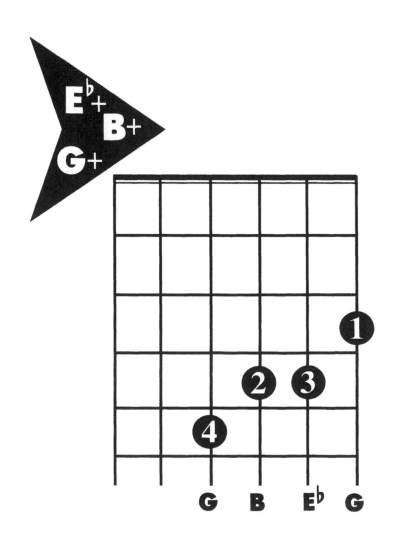

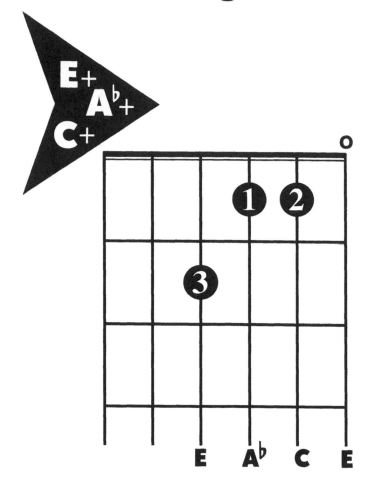

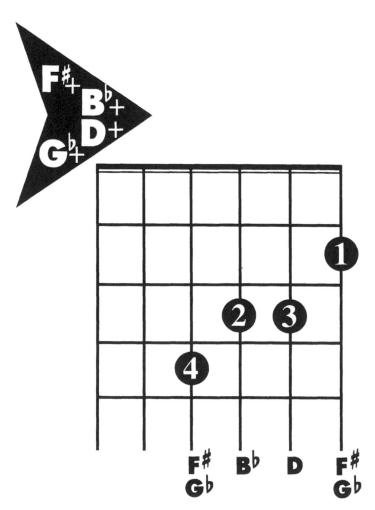

Sixth Chord (⁶)

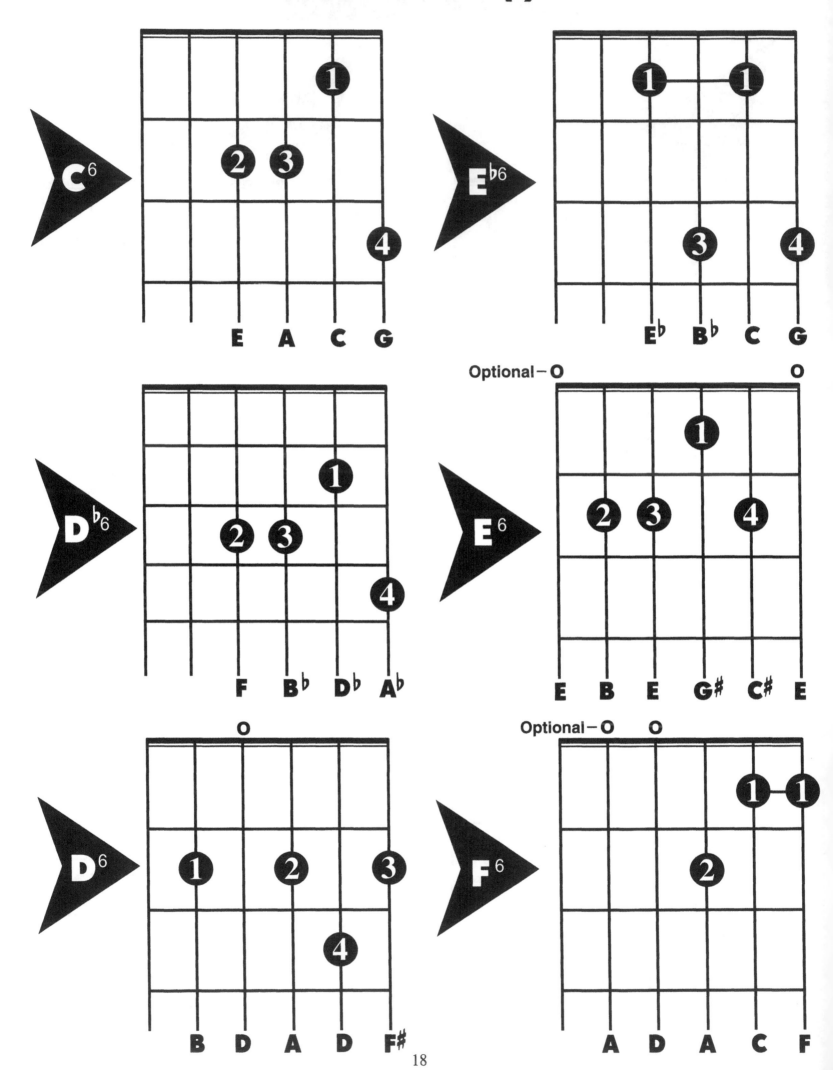

Sixth Chord (⁶)

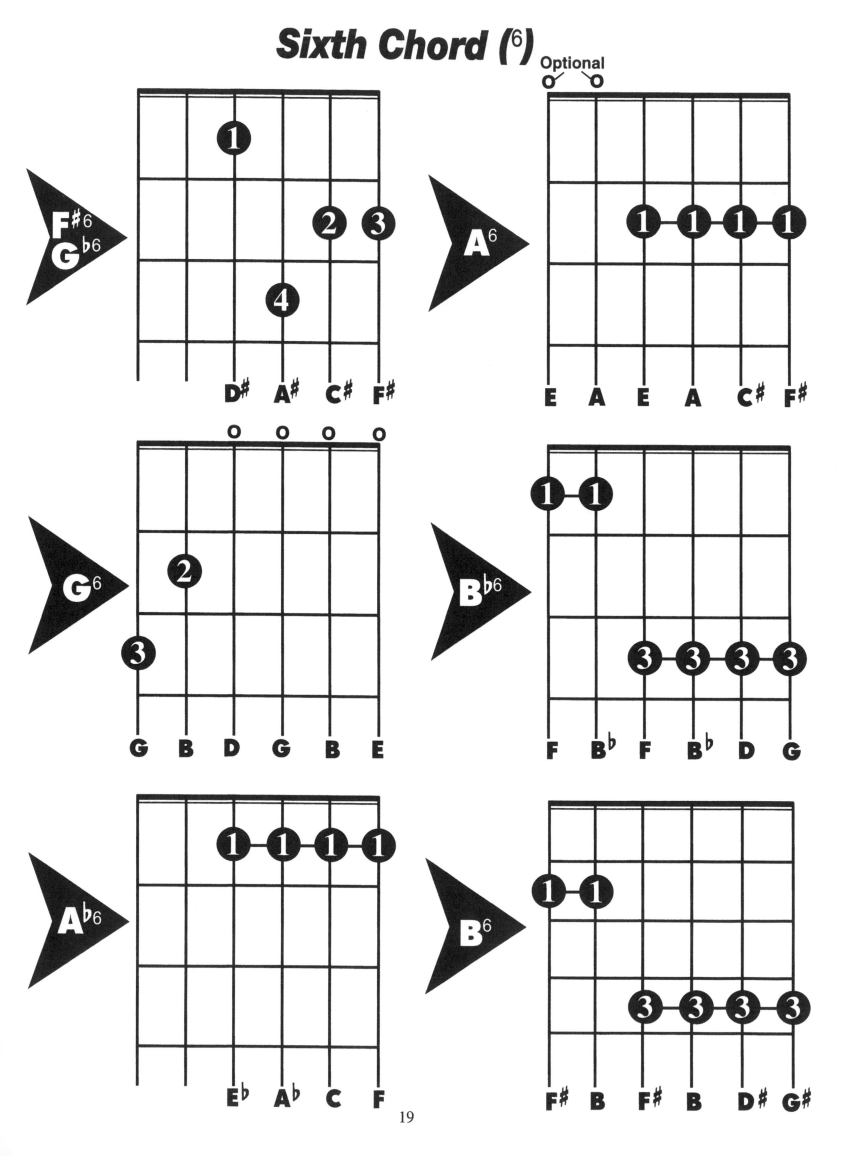

F#⁶ / G♭⁶

D# A# C# F#

A⁶ — Optional o o

E A E A C# F#

G⁶

G B D G B E

B♭⁶

F B♭ F B♭ D G

A♭⁶

E♭ A♭ C F

B⁶

F# B F# B D# G#

19

Minor Sixth (m⁶)

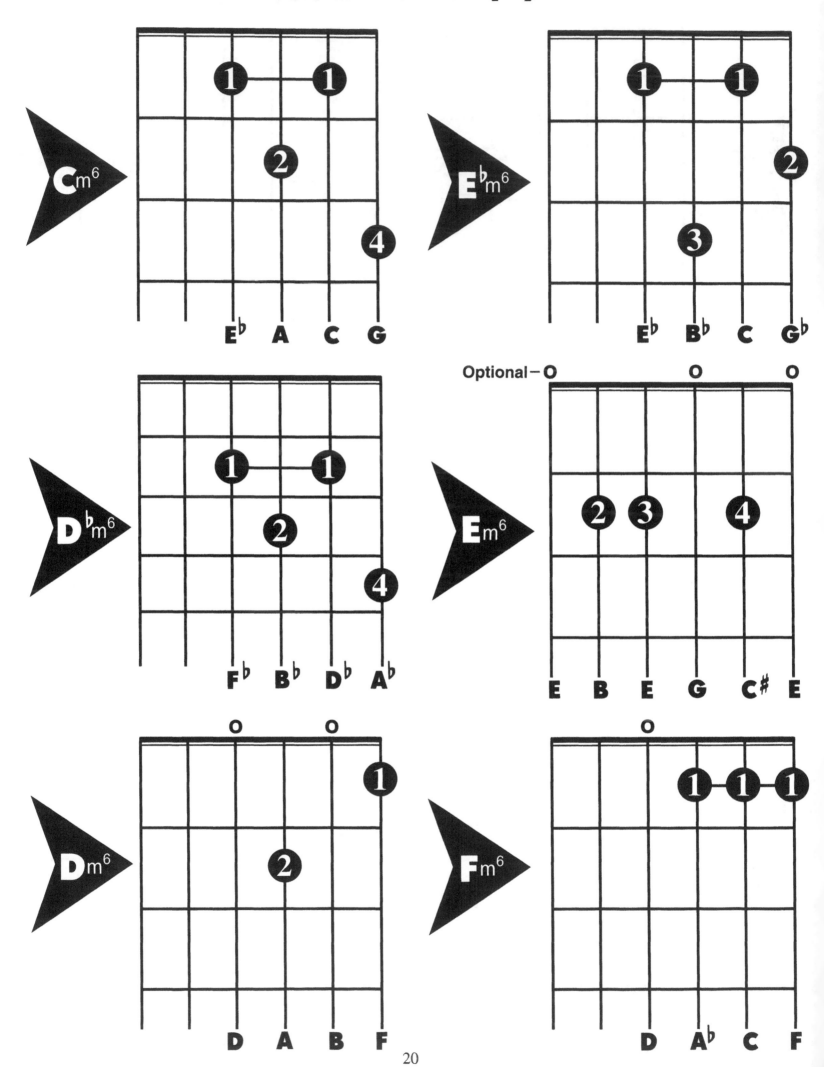

20

Minor Sixth (m⁶)

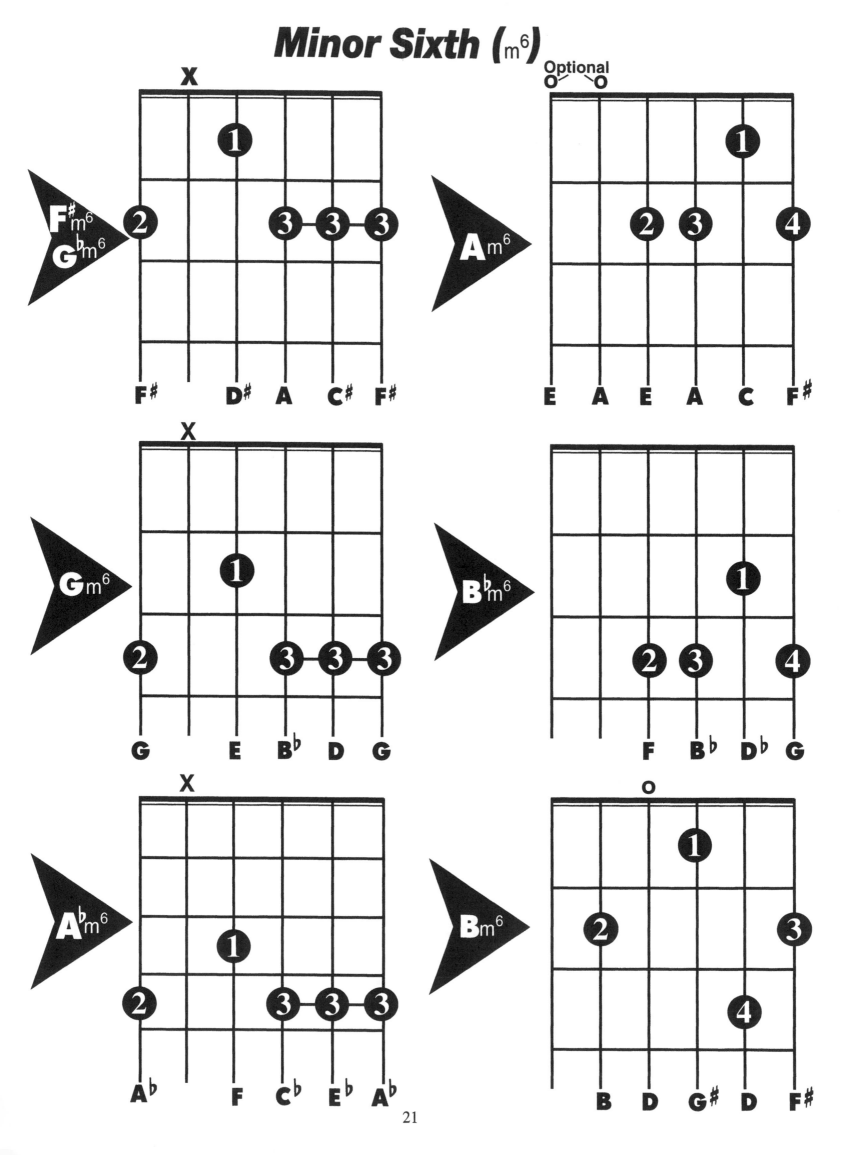

Major Seventh (ma⁷)

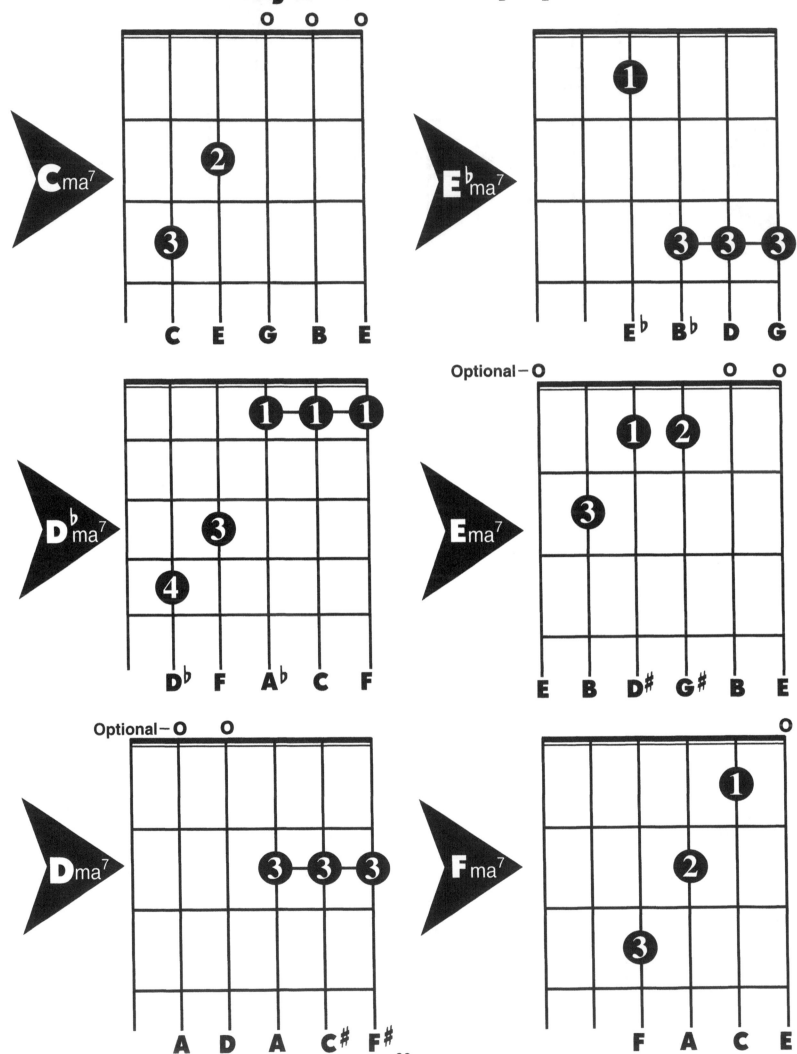

22

Major Seventh (ma7)

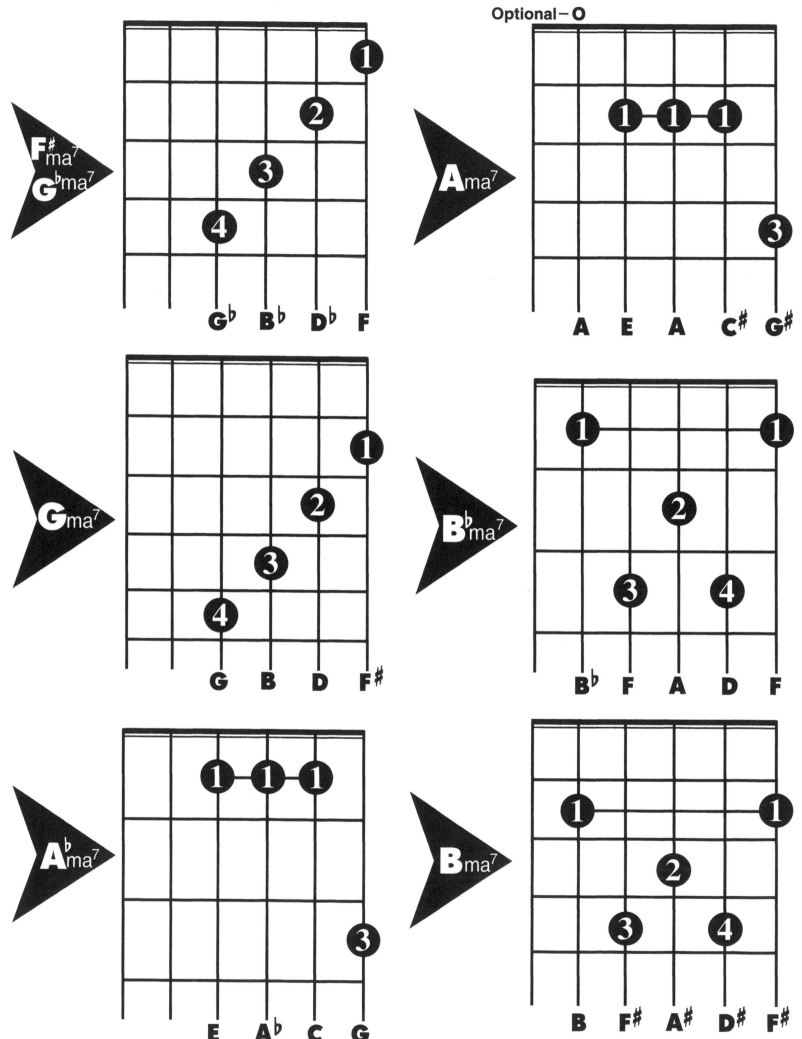

Minor Seventh (m⁷)

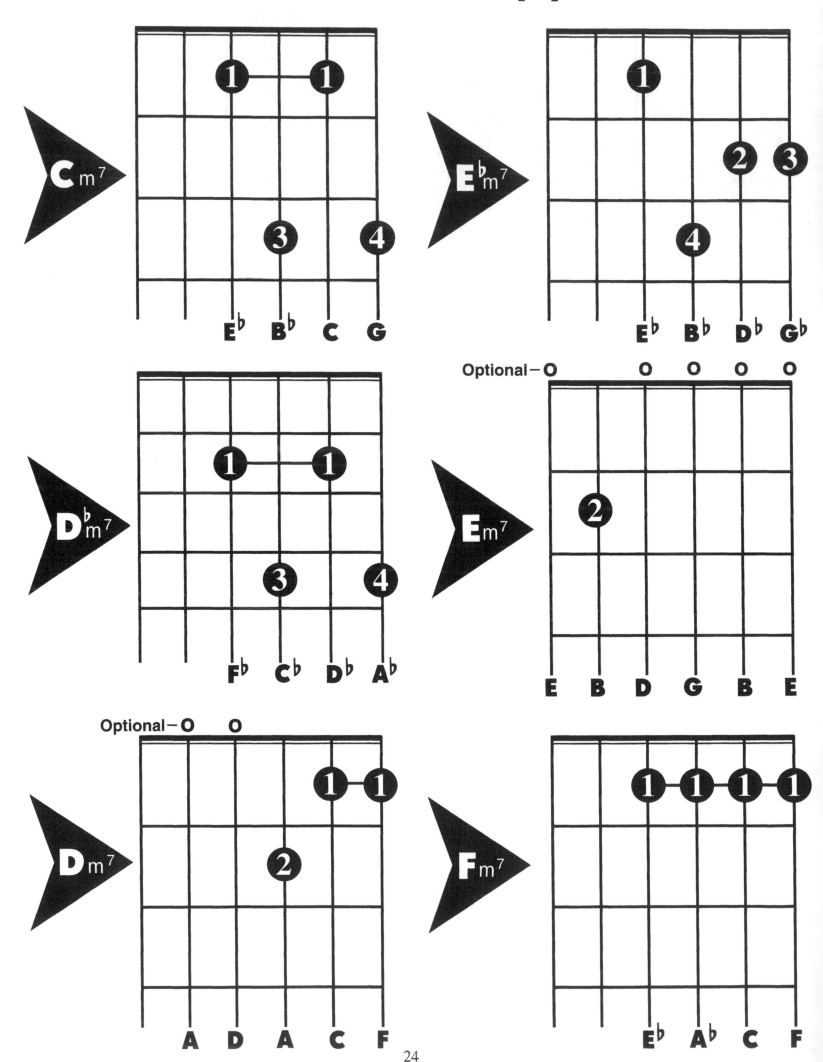

Minor Seventh (m7)

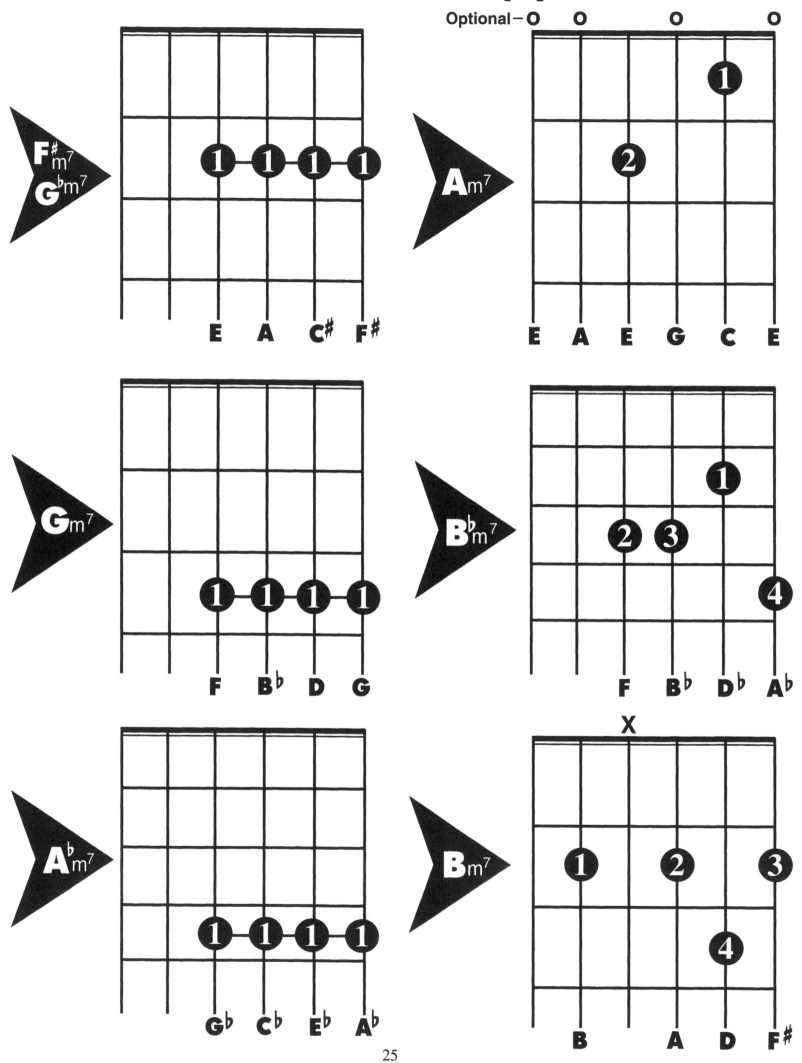

25

Seventh Dim. Fifth (⁷⁻⁵)

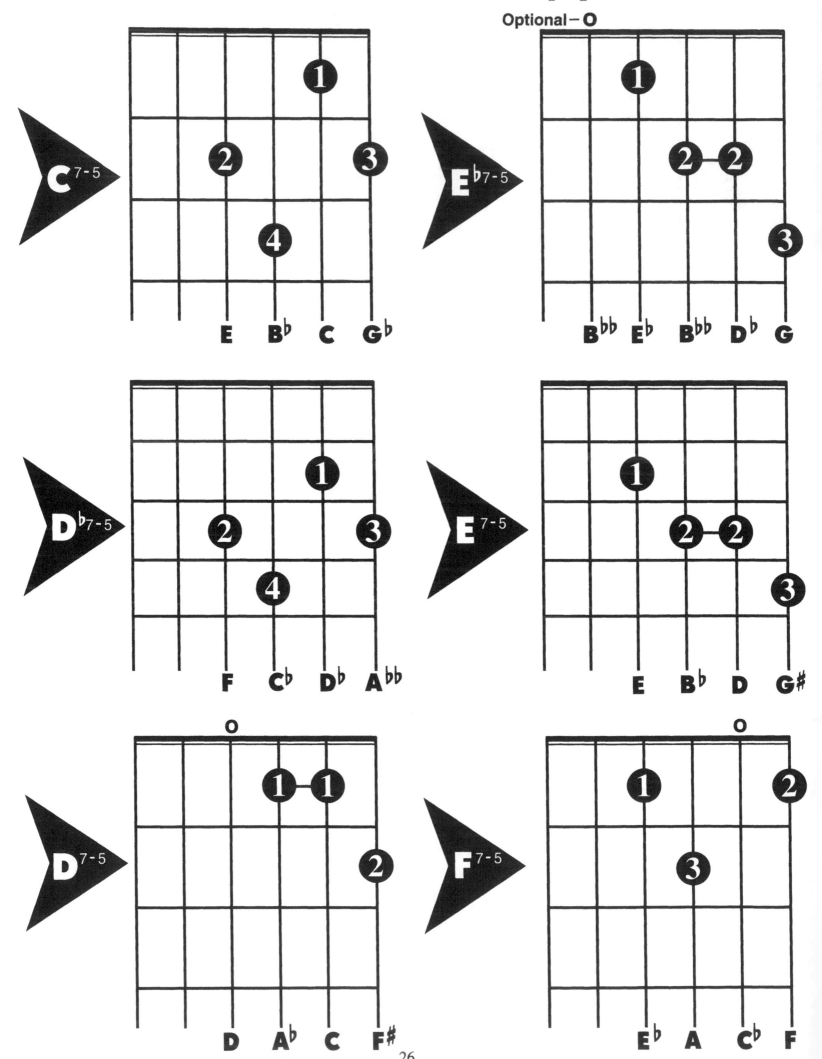

Seventh Dim. Fifth (7-5)

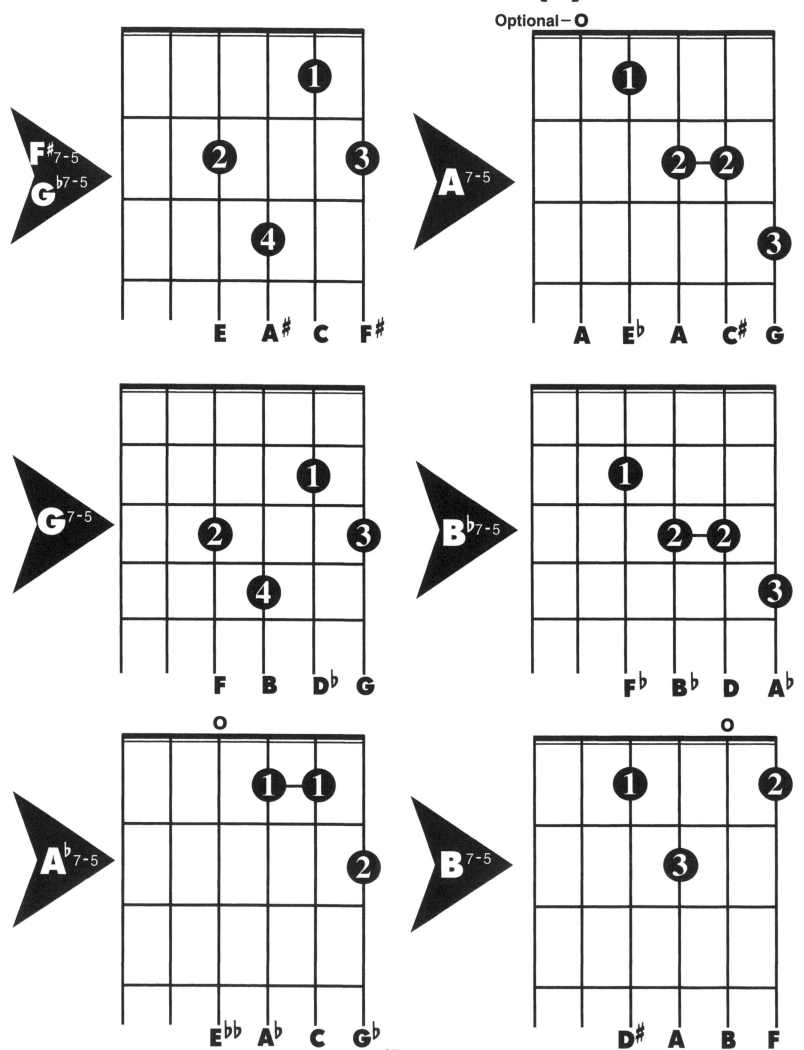

Seventh Aug. Fifth (7+5)

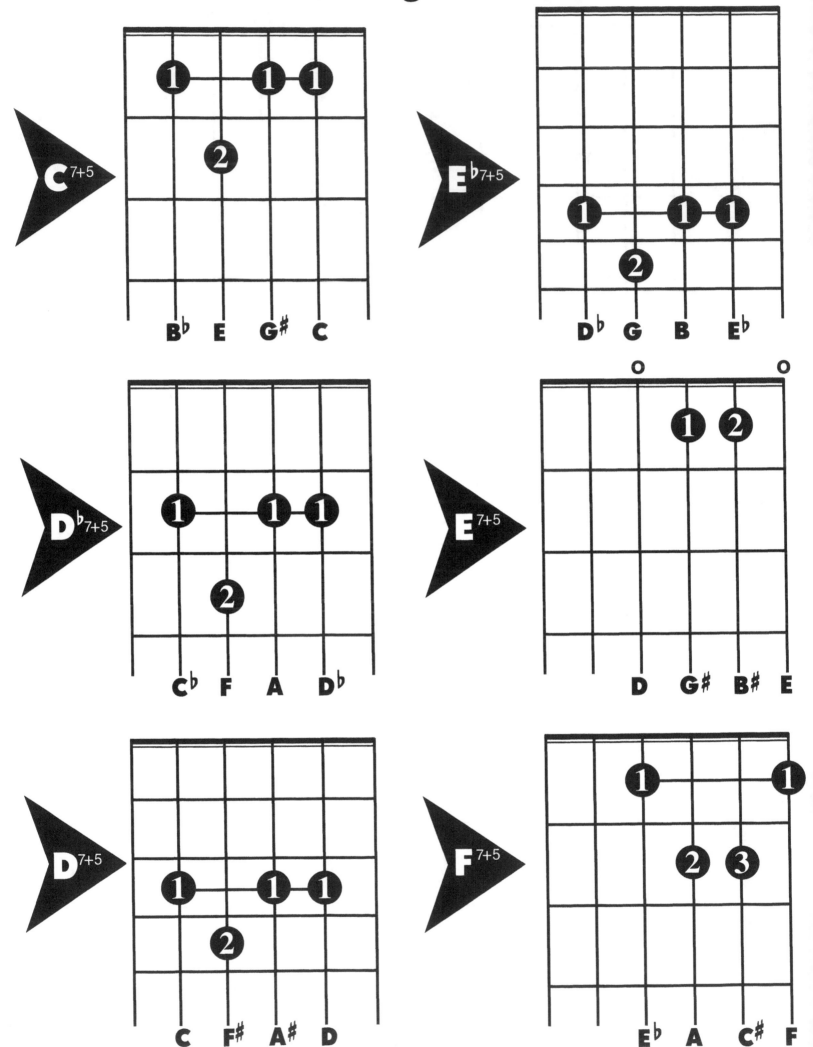

28

Seventh Aug. Fifth (7+5)

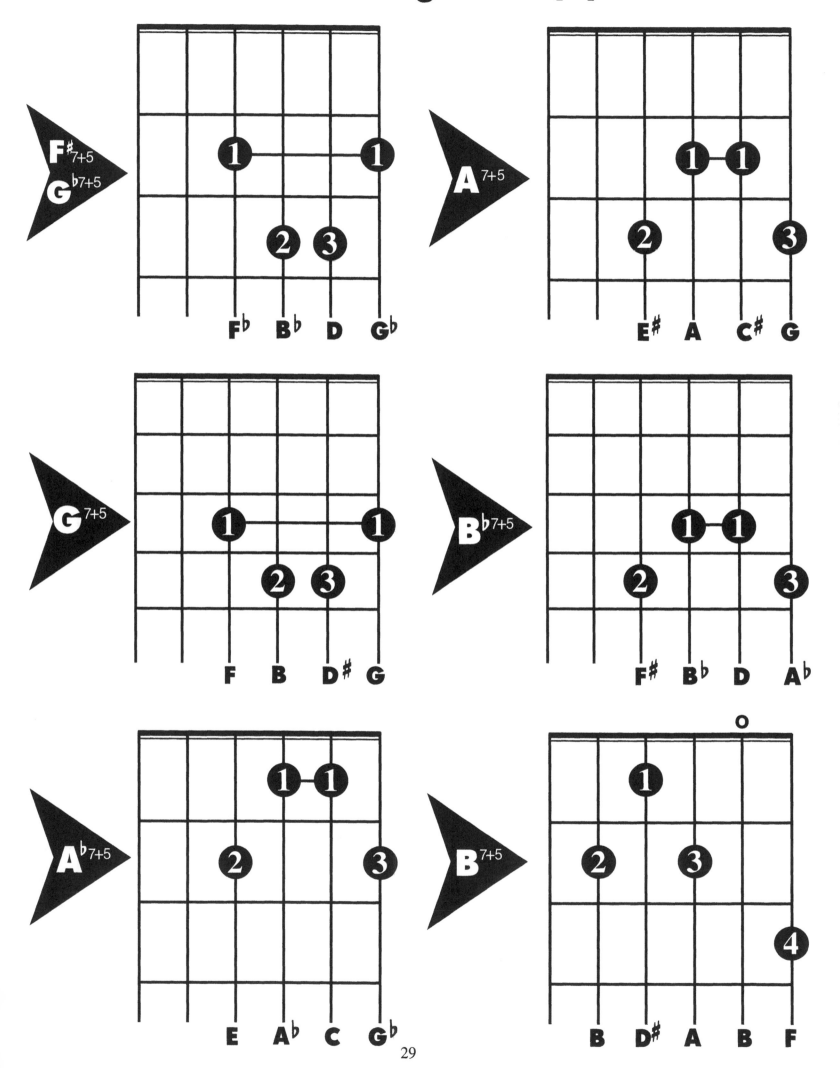

Ninth Chord (⁹)

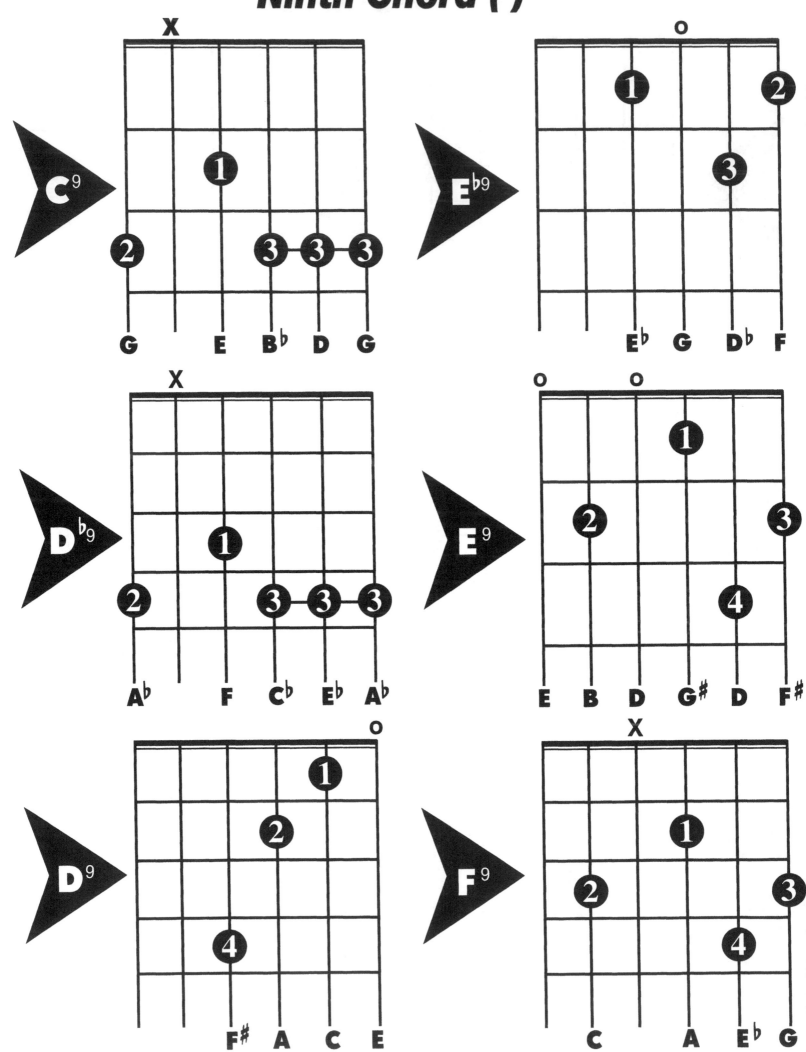

Ninth Chord (⁹)

F#⁹ / G♭⁹

X

C#   A#   E   G#

A⁹

Optional – O   O

E   A   E   B   C#   G

G⁹

O   O

D   A   B   F

B♭⁹

O

D   A♭   C   F

A♭⁹

E♭   B♭   C   G♭

B⁹

X

F#   D#   A   C#   F#

31

How to Transpose

TRANSPOSING is the method of changing from one key to another. Suppose the key of the song you want to sing is either too high or too low; perhaps another key would sound better on the guitar or you want to play chords that are easier with which to accompany another musical instrument.

The Transposing Chart

Key of	Key Signature	1	2	3	4	5	6	7	8	9	10	11	12
C	🎼	C	C♯	D	D♯	E	F	F♯	G	G♯	A	A♯	B
G	🎼♯	G	G♯	A	A♯	B	C	C♯	D	D♯	E	F	F♯
D	🎼♯♯	D	D♯	E	F	F♯	G	G♯	A	A♯	B	C	C♯
A	🎼♯♯♯	A	A♯	B	C	C♯	D	D♯	E	F	F♯	G	G♯
E	🎼♯♯♯♯	E	F	F♯	G	G♯	A	A♯	B	C	C♯	D	D♯
B	🎼♯♯♯♯♯	B	C	C♯	D	D♯	E	F	F♯	G	G♯	A	A♯
F♯	🎼♯♯♯♯♯♯	F♯	G	G♯	A	A♯	B	C	C♯	D	D♯	E	F
C♯	🎼♯♯♯♯♯♯♯	C♯	D	D♯	E	F	F♯	G	G♯	A	A♯	B	C
F	🎼♭	F	G♭	G	A♭	A	B♭	B	C	D♭	D	E♭	E
B♭	🎼♭♭	B♭	B	C	D♭	D	E♭	E	F	G♭	G	A♭	A
E♭	🎼♭♭♭	E♭	E	F	G♭	G	A♭	A	B♭	B	C	D♭	D
A♭	🎼♭♭♭♭	A♭	A	B♭	B	C	D♭	D	E♭	E	F	G♭	G
D♭	🎼♭♭♭♭♭	D♭	D	E♭	E	F	G♭	G	A♭	A	B♭	B	C
G♭	🎼♭♭♭♭♭♭	G♭	G	A♭	A	B♭	B	C	D♭	D	E♭	E	F

How To Use The Chart

A song is written in the key of "D" and it is too low. The chords in the song are "D", and "A7" and "G". You desire to play it higher, in the key of "G", for example. Simply find the line on the chart in the original key of "D", then match up the line in the key of "G".

EXAMPLE:

Key of "D"	to transpose to	Key of "G"
"D" Chord	becomes	"G" Chord
"A7" Chord	becomes	"D7" Chord *
"G" Chord	becomes	"C" Chord

* Don't be confused if a chord is an "A7". Transposing *only* changes the letter name of the chord while the extensions remain the same. For example, an **A7+5** becomes a **D7+5**.